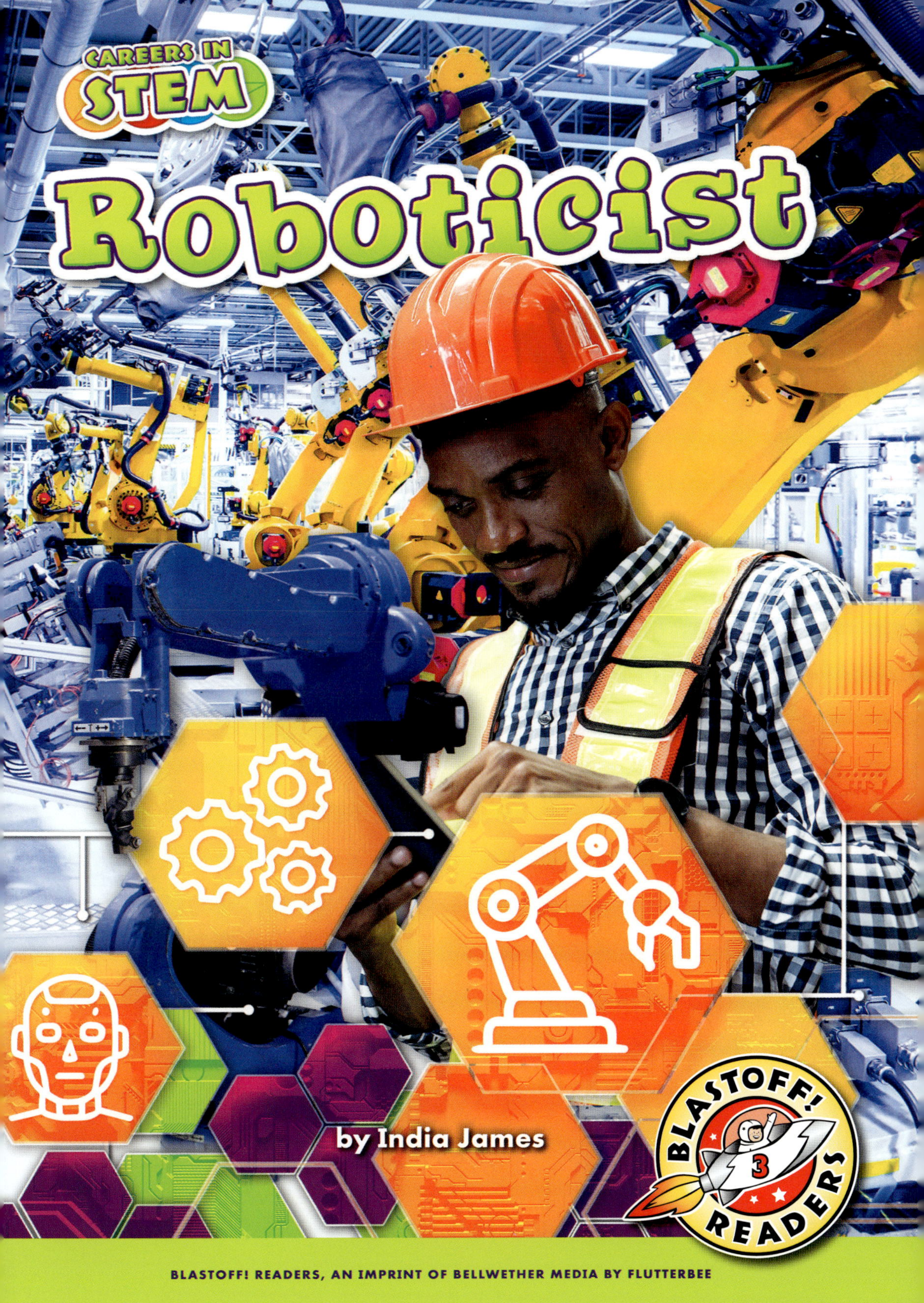
CAREERS IN STEM
Roboticist
by India James
BLASTOFF! READERS
3
BLASTOFF! READERS, AN IMPRINT OF BELLWETHER MEDIA BY FLUTTERBEE

Blastoff! Readers are carefully developed by literacy experts to build reading stamina and move students toward fluency by combining standards-based content with developmentally appropriate text.

Level 1 provides the most support through repetition of high-frequency words, light text, predictable sentence patterns, and strong visual support.

Level 2 offers early readers a bit more challenge through varied sentences, increased text load, and text-supportive special features.

Level 3 advances early-fluent readers toward fluency through increased text load, less reliance on photos, advancing concepts, longer sentences, and more complex special features.

★ **Blastoff! Universe**

Reading Level

Grade K

Grades 1–3

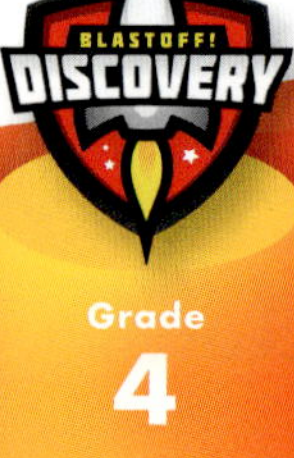

Grade 4

This edition first published in 2027 by Bellwether Media, Inc.

For information regarding permission, write to Bellwether Media, Inc., Attention: Permissions Department, 3500 American Blvd W, Suite 150, Bloomington, MN 55431.

Library of Congress Cataloging-in-Publication Data is available at www.loc.gov or upon request from the publisher.

ISBN: 9798898800789 (hardcover)
ISBN: 9798898802028 (ebook)

Editor: Betsy Rathburn Designer: Andrea Schneider

Printed in the United States of America, North Mankato, MN.

Table of Contents

Making a Robot

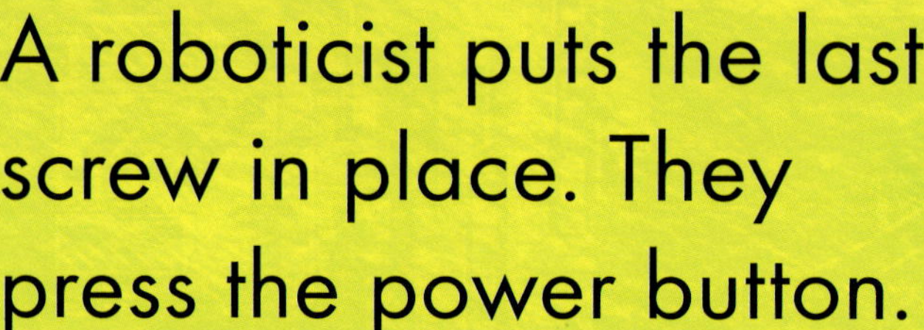

A roboticist puts the last screw in place. They press the power button.

Lights flash. Wheels spin. Arms start to wave. The robot is ready to work!

robot

What Is a Roboticist?

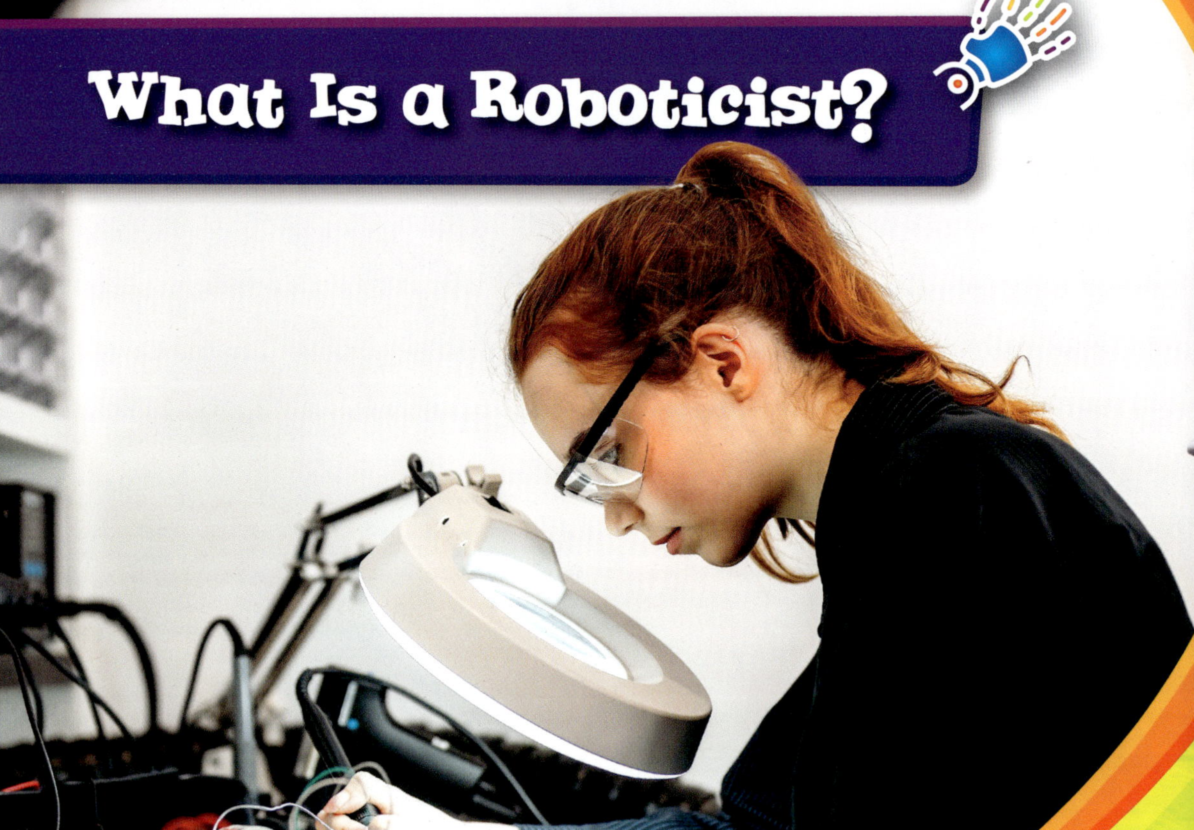

Roboticists **design** and build robots. They work on every part of a robot.

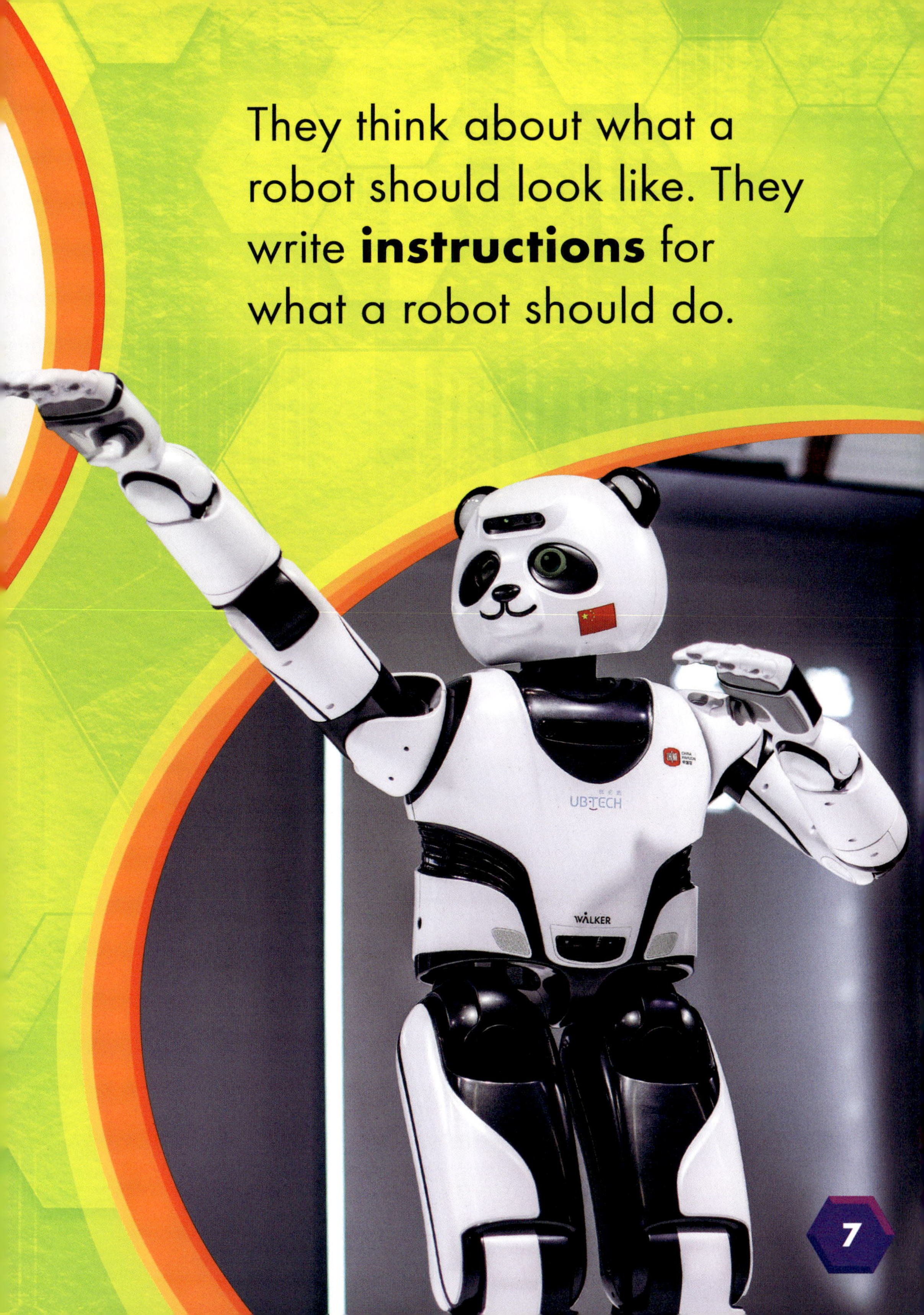

They think about what a robot should look like. They write **instructions** for what a robot should do.

Roboticists work in offices, **labs**, and factories. They make different types of robots.

Famous Roboticist

Name — Ruzena Bajcsy

Born — May 28, 1933

Birthplace — Bratislava, Slovakia

Schooling — Slovak Technical University; Stanford University

Known For — finding ways to help robots sense the world around them

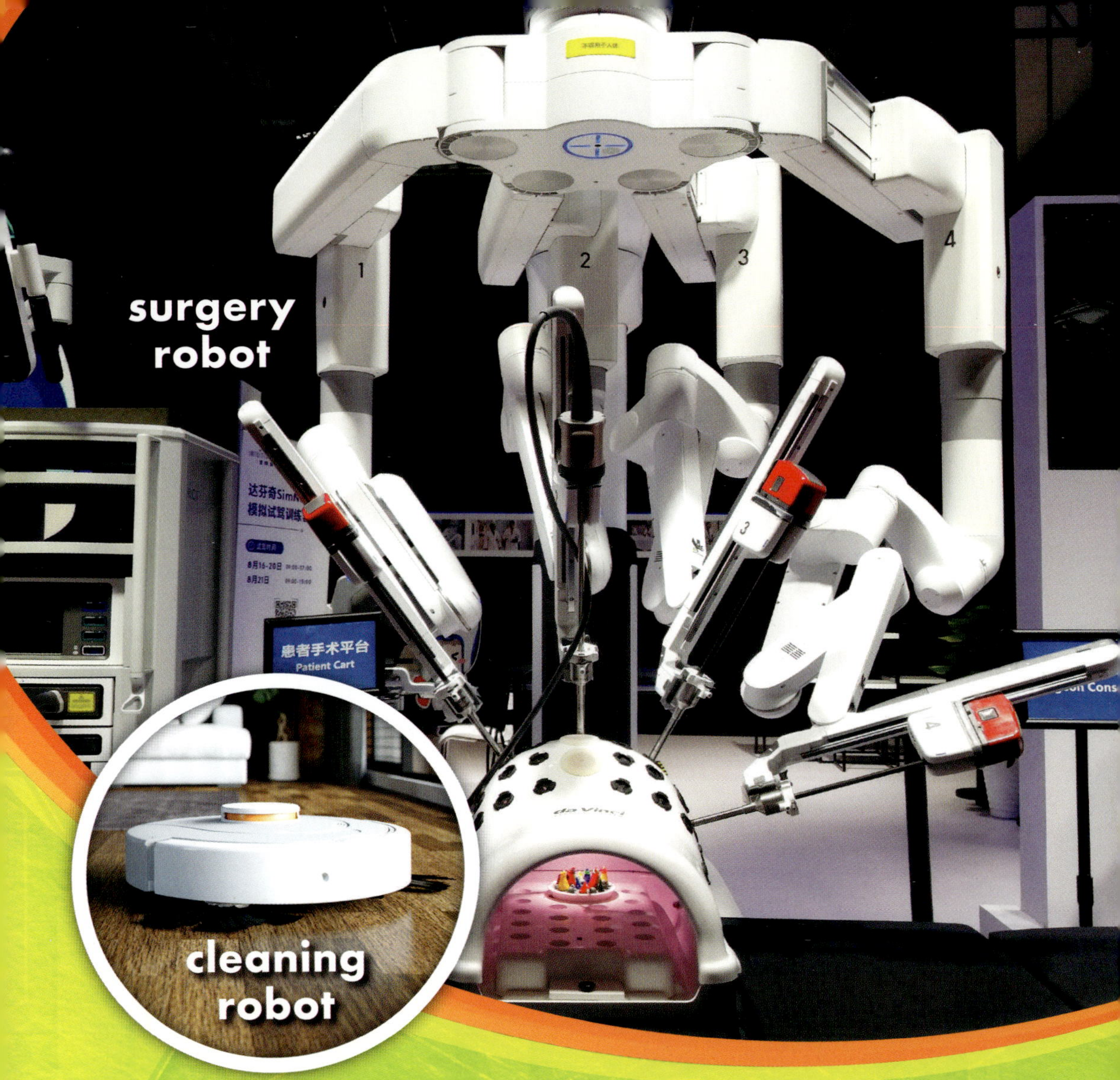

Some make robots that build things. Some make robots that clean houses. Some make robots that do **surgeries**!

At Work

Robots have many parts. They may have wheels, arms, or parts used to grab.

Some roboticists **engineer** these parts. They use computers to help design and **manufacture** the parts they need.

Robots need to be told what to do. Some roboticists write **code** to give robots instructions.

They also train robots using **artificial intelligence**. This helps robots learn from their mistakes.

Robotics in Real Life

safer factories to work in

robotic surgeries

more robots to help people

Robots have many wires. Some roboticists plan where wires should go.

Using STEM

answer questions by testing ideas

Technology

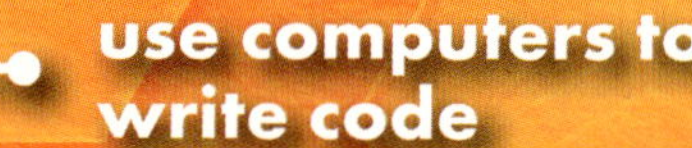

use computers to write code

build parts to make robots

plan how robots move

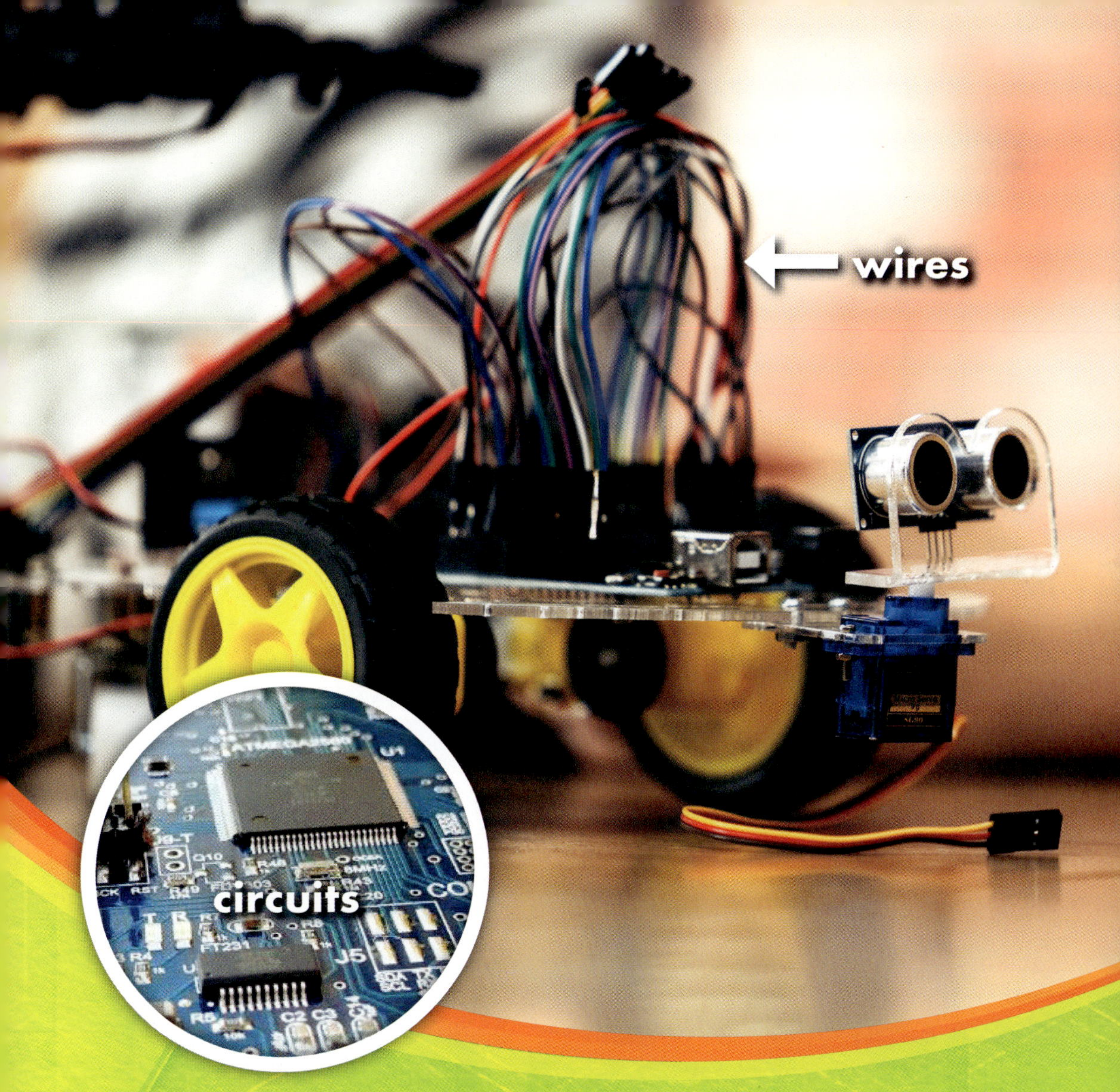

They also design **circuits** for robots. They make sure that every part of a robot can work with other parts.

Becoming a Roboticist

Roboticists usually go to college. They often study engineering or computer science.

Some learn to write code. Some study how to build parts. Some study electricity.

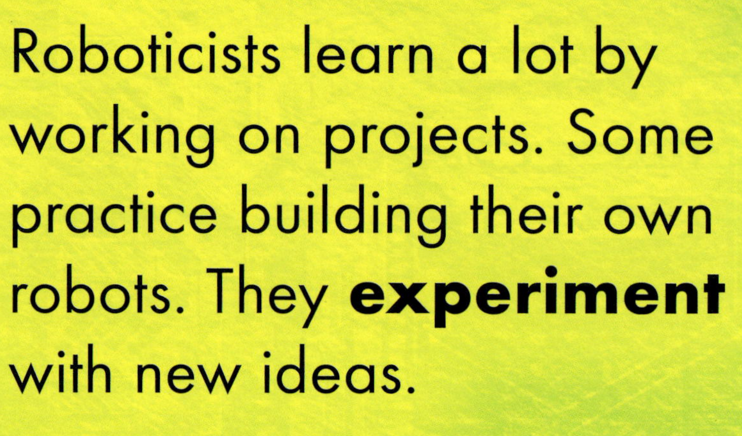

Roboticists learn a lot by working on projects. Some practice building their own robots. They **experiment** with new ideas.

They have many projects in school. They may also do **internships** to get experience.

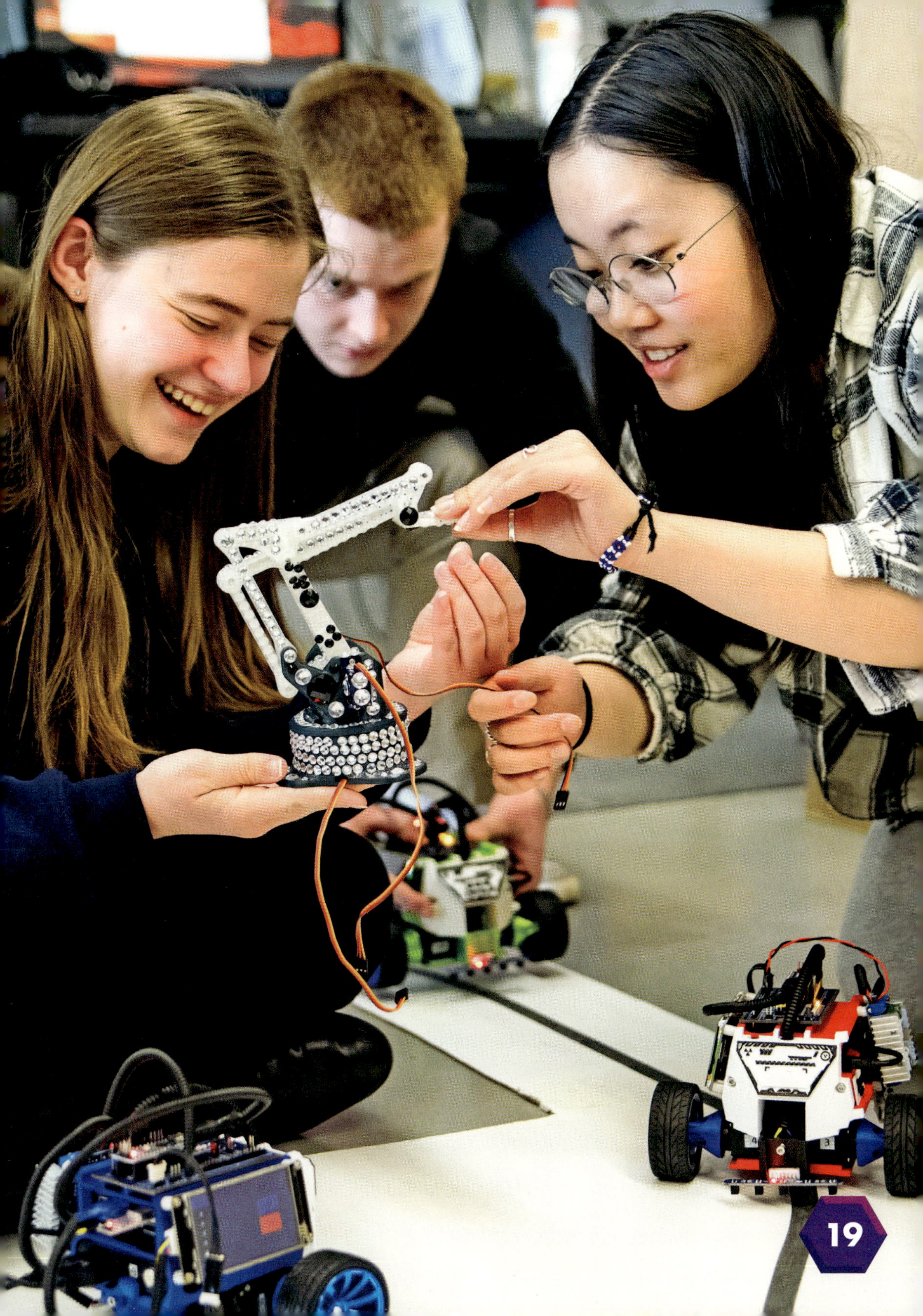

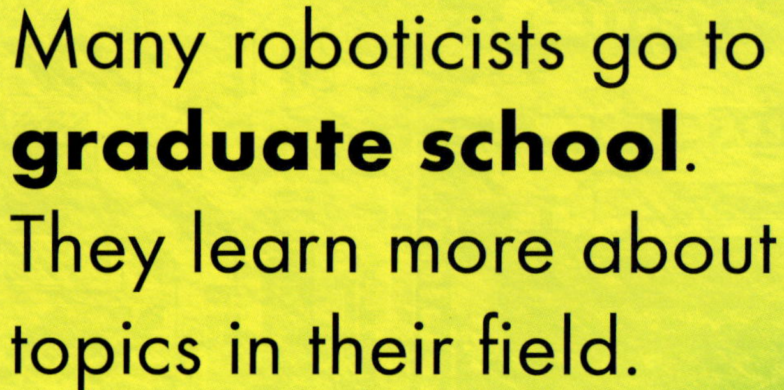

Many roboticists go to **graduate school**. They learn more about topics in their field.

How to Become a Roboticist

1. go to college
2. do projects with robots
3. complete an internship
4. find a job at an office, lab, or factory

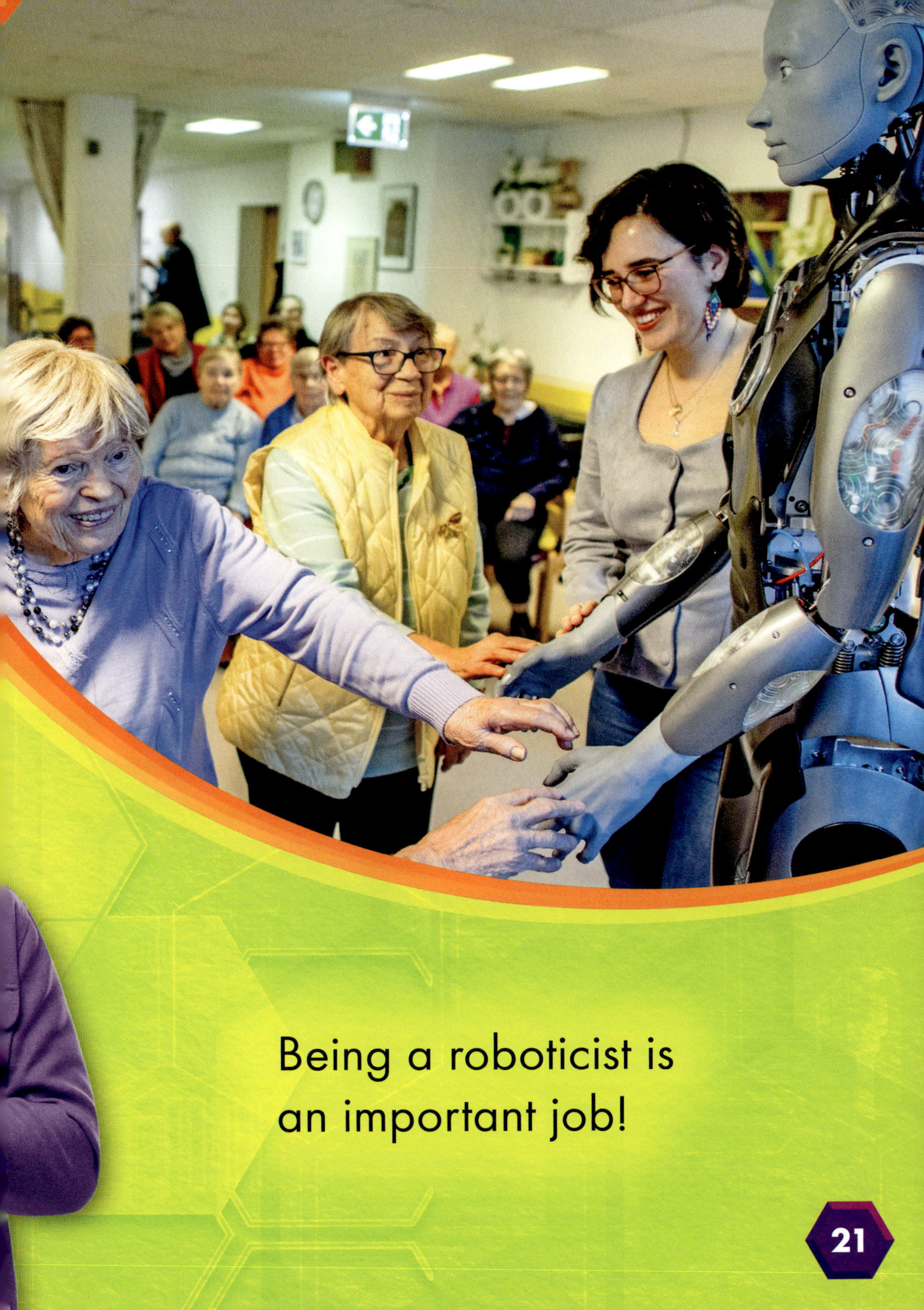

Being a roboticist is an important job!

Glossary

artificial intelligence—computer programs that imitate how humans make decisions

circuits—complete paths of electricity

code—instructions for a computer

design—to make a plan for a building, object, or pattern

engineer—to design and build machines, systems, or structures

experiment—to do tests to try new ideas or answer questions

graduate school—a school where people study a specialty area after college

instructions—a set of commands or procedures to follow

internships—programs in which people work at a job to gain work experience

labs—buildings or rooms with special tools to do science experiments and tests

manufacture—to turn raw materials into a final product

surgeries—medical procedures in which a doctor removes or repairs a part of the body

To Learn More

AT THE LIBRARY

Nargi, Lela. *Curious About Space Robots*. Mankato, Minn.: Amicus, 2024.

Spiro, Ruth. *How To Explain Robots To A Grown-Up*. Watertown, Mass.: Charlesbridge, 2024.

Terp, Gail. *Medical Robots*. Mankato, Minn.: Amicus, 2024.

ON THE WEB

FACTSURFER

Factsurfer.com gives you a safe, fun way to find more information.

1. Go to www.factsurfer.com.
2. Enter "roboticist" into the search box and click 🔍.
3. Select your book cover to see a list of related content.

Index

The images in this book are reproduced through the courtesy of: Amorn Suriyan, front cover (roboticist); FOTO Eak, front cover (robot); EyeEm Mobile GmbH, front cover (factory); Viru, p. 3; Makiko Tanigawa/ Getty Images, pp. 4 (robot), 4-5; PixeloneStocker/ Getty Images, pp. 6-7 (top); VCG/ Contributor/ Getty Images, pp. 7 (bottom), 8-9 (surgery robot); Franc Solina/ Wikipedia, p. 8 (Bajcsy); asbe, p. 9 (cleaning robot); Omer Messinger/ Stringer/ Getty Images, p. 10 (wheels, arm); Monty Rakusen/ Getty Images, pp. 10-11; European Commission/ Wikipedia, pp. 12-13; Jamie, p. 12 (code); imaginima, p. 13 (factories); Kemberly Groue/ Wikipedia, p. 13 (surgeries); Iparraguirre Recio/ Getty Images, p. 13 (help people); DJ Creative Studio, pp. 14-15 (wires); Farshadarvin/ Wikipedia, pp. 14-15 (circuits); martinedoucet, pp. 16-17 (top), 18-19; andresr, p. 17; Phynart Studio, p. 18 (inset); Damir Khabirov, pp. 20-21 (roboticist); picture alliance/ Contributor/ Getty Images, pp. 20-21 (top); Iryna, p. 23.